Warm up rou

Name the golfer according to the number of Major's won (as of August 2021).

Majors	Nationality	Turned Pro	Name
18	United States	1961	
15	United States	1996	
11	United States	1912	
9	United States	1919	
9	South Africa	1953	
8	United States	1971	
7	United States	1954	
7	United States	1931	
7	United States	1920	
7	United States	Never	
7	United States	1890	
6	England	1976	
6	United States	1992	
6	United States	1960	

Warm up round

Majors	Nationality	Turned Pro	Name
5	Spain	1974	
5	United States	1932	
5	Australia	1950	
5	England	1890	
5	Scotland	1896	
4	United States	1961	
4	South Africa	1989	
4	United States	Never	
4	South Africa	1938	
4	Northern Ireland	2007	
4	United States	2012	

Ryder Cup

1. Who is the player that stands atop the 17 and a half inch solid gold trophy that the winners receive?
a.   Bobby Jones b.   Samuel Ryder c.   Abe Mitchell

2. In which year did the Ryder Cup first take place?
a. 1907   b. 1917   c. 1927   d. 1937

3. In which year did it change from team GB&I to team Europe?
a. 1959   b. 1967   c. 1975   d. 1979

4. John Jacobs was the captain of Europe when their team first formed. There were 2 continental players in this team. Can you name them?

5. Which American blew Ian Woosnam off the course when he recorded a thumping 8&7 victory at the final day of the singles at Valderrama in 1997?

6. Who made the putt that retained the Ryder Cup for Europe at Medinah in 2012?

7. Who captained the United States to their dramatic 1999 victory?

8. Which golfer has won the most matches in Ryder Cup history?

9. Who was the last person to both captain and play for the US in the same Ryder Cup?

10. Who was the newly crowned Open champion and only rookie on the record making team to be included in the American team in 1981?
a. Bruce Lietzke   b. Tom Weiskopf   c. Bill Rogers

11. Which Welsh course hosted the Ryder Cup in 2010?

12. Which golf club in Louisville hosted the 2008 Ryder Cup?

13. Name the player that uncharacteristically broke his putter on the 6th hole at the 1987 Ryder Cup and had to putt the remaining holes with his 3 iron.

14. Name both of Nick Faldo's wildcard picks at the 2008 Ryder Cup.

15. Which of these players defeated Tiger Woods in the singles in 1997?

a. Constantino Rocca b. Darren Clarke c. Thomas Bjorn

16. In which year did Europe first win the Ryder Cup on American soil?

a. 1979 b. 1983 c. 1987 d. 1991

17. There have been a total of 6 aces at the Ryder Cup, but only one player has been able to close out the match that way. This player achieved this at the K Club in 2006. Name the player.

18. When were the United States last triumphant on European soil?

a. 1993 b. 1997 c. 2002 d. 2006

19. When did Europe and USA last tie the Ryder cup?

a. 1983 b. 1985 c. 1987 d. 1989

20. The 2002 Ryder Cup was poised at 8-8 after 2 days of impressive golf. What is the name of the Welshman who beat Phil Mickelson in Sunday's singles to help Europe edge a half point victory?

21. Which man defeated Jack Nicklaus in two singles matches both on the same day in 1975?
a. Brian Barnes   b. Brian Huggett   c. Peter Oosterhuis

22. Which pairing has played together the most at the Ryder Cup as of August 2021?

23. How many times has the Ryder Cup been held at the Belfry?

24. Name the US Ryder Cup captain that paired Tiger Woods and Phil Mickelson together at the 2004 Ryder Cup, which backfired spectacularly.

25. How many points did Nick Faldo contribute when Europe won the 1985 Ryder Cup?

26. What is the name of the oldest player to compete in the Ryder Cup? He was a captain's selection for the 1993 Ryder Cup at 51 years of age.
a. Lee Trevino   b. Ray Floyd   c. Lanny Watkins

27. At which venue did Jack Nicklaus first captain the United States?

28. In which year did Jack Nicklaus first captain the United States?

29. Who holds the record for the most Ryder Cup appearances from either team?

30. Name Europe's all-time best point scorer.

31. Which German last played in the Ryder Cup in 2002?

32. How old was Sergio Garcia when he became the youngest ever player to qualify as of right at the 1999 Ryder Cup?
a. 18   b. 19   c. 20   d. 21

33. What is the name of the European whose name was in the captain's envelope at the 1991 Ryder Cup, after Steve Pate was forced to retire with a rib injury?
a. Peter Baker   b. Steven Richardson   c. David Gilford

34. How big was team USA's lead at the start of the final day at the 'Miracle at Medinah'?

35. Name the 3 American players that won their singles on the Sunday at the 'Miracle at Medinah'.

36. Who was the young debutant at the 1977 Ryder Cup that went unbeaten in 4 outings?

37. Can you name the flamboyant Ryder Cup debutant that paired with Lee Westwood at the 2012 Ryder Cup that made 8 birdies and an eagle with his own ball to destroy Steve Stricker and Tiger Woods?

38. Who was the first Irishman to captain the Ryder Cup team?

39. How many singles points did team USA score on the final day at the 1999 Ryder Cup to secure a monumental comeback against Europe?
a. 8   b. 8.5   c. 9   d. 9.5

40. What is the name of the European rookie that got 4 points from 5 outings at the 2016 Ryder Cup?

Augusta

1. Who was the first winner of the Masters in 1934?

2. On which hole is the Hogan Bridge?

3. What is the name of the area where the rookie's stay at Augusta National?

4. How many times has an amateur finished runner up at the Masters as of August 2021?
a. 2   b. 3   c. 4   d. 5

5. What was strange about Zach Johnson's Masters win in 2007?

6. Which former US President was a member at Augusta, and famously had a tree named after him because he could never clear it with his tee shot?
a. Eisenhower   b. Nixon   c. Ford

7. Name the only two Englishmen to have ever won the Masters.

8. Weir and Mickelson won the Masters in 2003 and 2004. What do these two have in common making it the only time that is has ever happened?

9. In which year did McIlroy famously implode on the final day of the Masters?
a. 2009   b. 2010   c. 2011   d. 2012

10. Name the only South American to ever win the Masters (Bonus point if you get the year).

11. What is the collective name of holes 11,12 and 13?

12. The 2020 Masters saw the first player to break 70 in every round. What is the name of this player?

13. How many putts did Ernie Els infamously take when he made a 9 on the first hole in 2016?

14. True or false: Tiger Woods has led after round 1 at the Masters on multiple occasions.

15. In which year did the presentation of the green jacket begin?
a. 1942   b. 1949   c. 1955   d. 1959

16. What is the prize for getting an eagle at the Masters?

17. Arnold Palmer and Trevor Immelman share the record for the highest final-round score to win the masters. What score did they both get?
a. 73   b. 74   c. 75   d. 76

18. 8 golfers have won the Masters on 3 or more occasions. List them in order below: (1 point for every person in the correct position)

19. Gary Player was the first non-American player to win the Masters. Who was the second?

20. Who was the leading amateur player when Ian Woosnam won the Masters in 1991?
a. Mickelson   b. Els   c. Clarke   d. Westwood

21. Who did Nick Faldo famously overcome to win his third green jacket in 1996, where he shot an impressive 67 in the final round?

22. Who won the masters in 1988?

23. There were only 3 Americans in the top 10 of the 2017 Masters. Who was the leading American?
a. Rickie Fowler   b. Jordan Spieth   c. Matt Kuchar

24. How many times did Greg Norman finish in the top 3 of the Masters?
a. 5   b. 6   c. 7   d. 8

25. Which country was 2003 Masters winner Mike Weir from?

26. Danny Willett ended up winning by 3 shots at the 2016 Masters, but how many shots behind Spieth was he with 7 holes to play?
a. 4   b. 5   c. 6   d. 7

27. How many times have non-American golfers won the Masters?
a. 14   b. 17   c. 20   d. 22

28. What was the fourth hole at Augusta called before it was called "Flowering Crabapple"?
a. The Fern   b. The Palm   c. The Flower   d. The Apple

29. Complete the classic John Daly quote. "I've heard the winner of the Masters hosts the dinner. If I ever won it there would be no suits, no ties, and _____."
a. Unlimited bar   b. Casino   c. Mcdonalds   d. No pants

30. What use did Augusta National have during the Second World War? (not golf related)

31. In the last 10 years, how many times has there been no American golfer in the top 3?

32. How old was Guan Tianlang when he became the youngest player ever to make the cut at the 2013 Masters?

33. What was notable about Nicklaus' 1986 Masters win?

34. The 1980's are fondly remembered by the Europeans for their golfing success. How many Masters did the Europeans win during this decade?
a. 3   b. 4   c. 5   d. 6

35. Across the history of the Masters, which hole has proven to be the hardest according to score to par?

36. Tiger Woods' chip in at the 16th is considered by many to be the greatest golf shot of all time. In which year did this shot occur?
a. 2002   b. 2003   c. 2004   d. 2005

37. Following on from question 36, who did Tiger beat in a playoff to win the Masters?

38. What score did Matsuyama achieve when he won the 2021 Masters?
a. -7   b. -9   c. -10   d. -12

39. Who won the Green Jacket in 2000?

40. Dustin Johnson achieved the lowest finishing score in Masters history in 2020. What score did he finish with?
a. -18   b. -19   c. -20   d. -21

Tiger Woods

1. What is Tiger's full name?

2. What is the largest winning margin of Tiger's career?
a. 10   b. 12   c. 15   d. 17

3. Tiger holds the record for the most 5 plus tournament wins in a single season. How many 5 wins plus seasons has he had?
a. 8   b. 10   c. 12   d. 14

4. Tiger has only lost in one playoff in his career. What is his playoff record?
a. 8-1   b. 9-1   c. 10-1   d. 11-1

5. Who is the only person to beat Tiger in a playoff?
a. Phil Mickelson   b. Ernie Els   c. Billy Mayfair

6. Tiger emerged straight away as a star on the PGA tour. How many PGA starts did it take him to win his first tournament?
a. 3rd   b. 5th   c. 7th   d. 9th

7. Who did Tiger defeat when he won his first playoff on the PGA tour?
a. David Love III   b. Tom Lehman   c. Ed Fiori

8. In which year did Tiger achieve the 'Tiger Slam', where he became the only player to win 4 consecutive majors?
a. 2000   b. 2001   c. 2002   d. 2003

9. Which course did Tiger win his 1st of 3 U.S. Junior Amateurs, where he would later win 8 PGA Tour titles?
a. Doral   b. Firestone   c. Bay Hill   d. Torrey Pines

10. Which player has Tiger finished runner up to the most in all PGA Tour events?

11. Tiger finished runner up every time this player won a PGA title. Which player is this?
a. Rich Beem   b. Bart Bryant   c. Trevor Immelman

12. What was Tiger's first PGA tour event?

13. At which course did Tiger achieve his greatest winning margin?

14. What was Tiger's career low round on the PGA tour?
a. 59   b. 60   c. 61   d. 62

15. What is the longest winning streak (consecutive tournament wins) of Tiger's career? (Bonus question which player has the longest?)
a. 4   b. 5   c. 6   d. 7

16. Tiger holds the record for the greatest number of weeks at the top of the Official World Rankings. How many weeks was this?
a. 416 weeks   b. 572 weeks   c. 683 weeks   d. 809 weeks

17. At which tournament did Tiger's impressive stat of 142 consecutive cuts made end?
a. 2006 U.S Open   b. 2005 At&T Byron Nelson
c. 2007 Open Championships   d. 2010 Players Championships

18. How long was Tiger's first tenure at world number 1?
a. 1 week   b. 10 weeks   c. 22 weeks   d. 47 weeks

19. In 1996 Tiger won the NCAA Championships by 4 shots. What score did he shoot in the fnal round?
a. 62   b. 64   c. 78   d. 80

20. Which of these tournaments has Tiger not won 5 or more times?
a. PGA Championship   b. BMW Championship
c. Memorial Tournament Presented by Mastercard
d. Arnold Palmer Invitational presented by Mastercard

21. In which year did Tiger win the Masters by 12 shots?
a. 1995   b. 1997   c. 2000   d. 2003

22. Dustin Johnson has 6 World Golf Championship wins putting him in second place behind Tiger. How many WGC wins does Tiger have?
a. 8   b. 11   c. 14   d. 18

23. How many PGA tournaments has Tiger Woods won as of AUgust 2021?
a. 82   b. 88   c. 95   d. 111

24. How old was Tiger when he became the youngest player to win the Grand Slam?
a. 22   b. 24   c. 25   d. 26

25. Who did Tiger replace as the world number 1 when he first did so?

26. What percent of starts has Tiger won on the PGA Tour?
a. 15.8%   b. 18.3%   c. 22.8%   d. 27.1%

27. To the nearest 1 million dollars, what is Tiger's career prize money as of August 2021?
a. 98 million b. 121 million c. 147 million d. 182 million

28. When holding the outright lead going into the final day, what is Tiger's winning record?
a. 38-5 b. 48-4 c. 44-2 d. 56-5

29. Tiger only played 6 tournaments in the 2008 season before his season ended due to knee surgery, finishing second once. How many times did he win?
a. 0 b. 1 c. 3 d. 4

30. Out of the 76 rounds that Tiger played in the year 2000, how many of them were over par?
a. 0 b. 4 c. 8 d. 12

Golf Terminology

1. What is it called when a player gets 3 under par on a single hole?

2. When putting, what is the allowance that is made for a slope called?

3. What do you shout if your shot is in danger of hitting someone else? (Correct spelling needed)

4. What is it called when a player's ball lies directly in front of another player's ball on the green, and that player is not awarded relief?

5. What is the universally used golf grip called, where the little finger of the right hand overlaps the forefinger of the left hand?

6. What is the distance from where a shot is played, to the spot where it first lands, called?

7. What is the player playing first off the tee said to have?

8. A player playing off a zero handicap is known as what sort of golfer?

9. What is another term for a hole in one?

10. What is it called when you redo a poor shot without a stroke penalty?

11. Who oversees taking care of a golf course?

12. What is the curve that a ball takes when putting called?

13. What is a classic seaside golf course that is built near the mouth of a river called?
a. Chains   b. Moorland   c. Links   d. Parkland

14. What is the scoring format where players are awarded points for each hole, where achieving a par relative to their handicap gets you 2 points?

15. This is a game where each player in the team (usually a team of 4) tees off. The best ball is chosen, and all 4 players then play their shots from this position.

16. This game is **very** similar to question 15 but adds some new requirements. The team must take at least 4 tee shots from each player to avoid taking the better player's shot every time.

17. If a player wins the hole outright then they win the _____. If it is a tie, then the **value** of the _____ gets added to the next hole and winner of the next hole gets twice the amount of _____. What is this game mode called?

18. What do you call the place and position where a ball rests?

19. What do you call the movement of the club away from the ball before you hit it?

20. What is it called when you hit the turf in front of your ball, creating a big divot and causing the ball not to go **very** far?

Guess the Golfer

1. This Spanish golfer was born on the 10th of November 1994 and finished 3rd at the Open Championship in 2021.

2. This Mexican golfer was born on the 27th of February 1991. He won his first PGA title at the 2021 WGC-FedEx St. Jude Invitational.

3. This is a former world number 1 golfer that was born in 1971. He won the 1999 Players Championship and the 2001 Open Championship.

4. This American golfer turned pro in 2015. He finished second at both the 2018 Open Championships and the 2019 Masters and won gold at the 2020 Olympics.

5. This American golfer was born in 1958. He won PGA Tour events, including the 1983 PGA Championship.

6. This is an English golfer who was born in 1991. He has 6 European Tour victories and won the 2020 Arnold Palmer Invitational. He was part of the winning 2018 Ryder Cup team.

7. This player was nicknamed 'The Big Fijian'.

8. This tall golfer turned pro in 2007. He has finished in the top 2 of 9 PGA events but only managed to win one.

9. This Australian golfer was born in 1993. He won the 2017 Zurich Classic of New Orleans with Jonas Blixt and won the same tournament again with Marc Leishman in 2021.

10. This American player, born in 1970, has a very unorthodox swing. He holds the record for the lowest score in PGA Tour history with a round of 58.

11. This American golfer was born in 1955. He won consecutive U.S Open titles and is a member of the golf hall of fame. He topped the money list in 1985, 1987 and 1988.

12. This Norwegian golfer, born in 1997, won the 2021 BMW International Open.

13. This Swedish golfer was born in 1965 and spent 38 weeks in the world's top 10 in 2000 and 2001. He finished second in the 1994 and 1997 Open Championship, and 5th at the 1996 PGA Championship.

14. This golfer became world number one on May the 13th 2018.

15. Contrary to what his surname might suggest, this player is not English.

16. This American golfer, born in 1960, won twelve times on the PGA Tour, including the 1993 PGA Championship.

17. This golfer reached a career high ranking of 5th in 2008. He defeated Tom Watson in a 4-person playoff at the 2009 Open Championship.

18. This golfer spent nearly 200 weeks in the top 10 of the world rankings from 1986-2000. He was the PGA Player of the Year in 1998, which is the same year that he won 2 Majors.

19. This golfer was ranked the number 1 amateur golfer in the world for 55 weeks until he turned pro in 2012. He has 4 wins on the PGA Tour and came 3rd at the 2019 PGA Championship.

20. This Zimbabwean golfer was born in 1957. He won 3 Majors including two victories at the PGA Championship in 1992 and 1994.

21. This golfer is famous for shushing the European crowd at the Ryder Cup.

22. This golfer won the 2018 Players Championship.

23. This English golfer, born in 1973, is well known for his consistency.

24. This golfer broke his putter at the 2021 Masters and had to putt with his 3 wood.

25. This young American golfer came second at the 2021 Masters.

26. This man became the first Dane to qualify for the Ryder Cup.

27. This American golfer turned pro in 1979. He won 3 Majors before sadly dying in an airplane accident at the age of 42.

28. This 6 ft 4-inch American golfer turner pro in 2008. He has 2 PGA Tour wins, with the most recent coming at the 2021 Charles Schwab Challenge.

29. This golfer was rookie of the year for the 2018/2019 PGA Tour and got his first PGA win at the Honda Classic in 2020.

30. This Canadian golfer finished 8th at the 2021 Masters.

Anagram Round

The following 20 anagrams will be current or past golfers.

1. jr monah

2. cabrera haman

3. akim ftp tract zit

4. anosmic therm

5. aachen byrom bused

6. gran monger

7. eleni ser

8. ape bork kooks

9. monilia warlock

10. cd reposeful

11. alick fond

12. donnish juntos

13. abramo azaleas joli

14. elihu ut zoonosis

15. coyly mirror

16. jag ny shiv

17. alic cask junk

18. adham amitie yuks

19. aachen duffs lexer

20. dow goiters

The following **10** anagrams will be famous golf courses. Golf club will be omitted from the titles of the clubs to make it slightly easier.

1. dans wrest

2. evelin play

3. aaas ainu glutton

4. cory snippets

5. cellini conks shh

6. acton roundly yow

7. Acton koruny tom

8. Filide rum

9. emir no

10. henri puts

General Knowledge

1. Which Major is Rory McIlroy yet to win as of August 2021?

2. Who became the first European to score what is now known as the maximum number of 5 points in a Ryder Cup, which happened in 2018?

3. What is the maximum amount of time that a golfer can take to look for a lost ball?
a. 2 mins   b. 3 mins   c. 4 mins   d. 5 mins

4. What is the maximum number of clubs that a golfer can bring with them on their round?

5. Name the two golfers that have been world number 1 without winning a Major.

6. True or false: a ball that rests nestled between the flagstick and the hole counts as being in the hole.

7. Name the five defined areas on a golf course.

8. Golf reappeared at the Olympics in 2016. When was it last in the Olympics before that date?
a. 1904   b. 1920   c. 1952   d. 1964

9. Who was at the top of the world rankings before the Coronavirus lockdown started?

10. Who was the only non-American golfer to win a Major in 2019?

11. Excluding the Tour Championship, what is the most lucrative event on tour?

12. What is the total prize pool from question 11?
a. $15 million   b. $17.5 million   c. $20 million

13. Which player stunned the golfing world by winning the 2003 PGA Championship, despite only being ranked 169th in the world?

14. What was Tiger's world ranking when he won the 2019 Masters?
a. 6   b. 8   c. 10   d. 12

15. Royal St George's Golf Club is based in which English town, that also shares its name with a popular lunchtime meal?

16. Where is golf said to have originated?

17. There are only 4 players that have made an albatross at the Masters. Try and name all 4.

18. When does the St Andrews old course date back to?
a. 1387   b. 1454   c. 1552   d. 1661

19. Who was the first golfer to make a televised hole-in-one?

20. 10 golfers spent the entirety of the 2010s within the top 100 of the golf world rankings. How many can you name? (1 point for every correct answer)

21. Which golfer won 7 straight European Tour Order of Merit titles from 1993-1999?

22. Which country was Justin Rose born in?

23. Who became the first male player born in Asia to win a Major when he lifted the 2009 PGA Championship, where he also became the first player to come from behind to beat Tiger in the final day of a Major.

24. Put the following players in order of most to least European Tour victories: Padraig Harrington, Tiger Woods, Ernie Els, Miguel Angel Jimenez. (1 point for 2 correct answers and 2 points for 4 correct answers)

25. There are 5 players who have finished within the top 5 of all 4 Majors in a calendar year. Who are they? (1 point for every correct answer)

26. 4 different golfers began the 21st century as reigning Major champions. Who are they? (1 point for every correct answer)

27. As of August 2021, who are the last Major winners from these 5 countries? (1 point for the correct name, for the correct Major and the correct year)

USA
England
Australia
Northern Ireland
South Africa

28. In which country can one find the 13th Beach Golf Links, that hosted a 2019 European Tour event?

29. Which South African became the first golfer in history to shoot an 8 under 62 in a Major at the 2017 Open Championship?

30. Which Swedish golfer, who retired in 2008, is widely regarded as the greatest female golfer of all time?

31. Which golfer summed up his playoff loss to Jack Nicklaus at the 1991 U.S Senior Open with "the bear crushed the mouse"?

32. Between the years of 1966-1980 Jack Nicklaus had an incredible record at the British Open. What was his worst finish over this time?
a. 4th   b. 6th   c. 8th   d. 10th

33. Which is the only Major that Lee Trevino never won?

34. How many 18-hole rounds must a golfer submit in order to get an official handicap in the USA?

35. Which number did John Daly give to his iron that he started teeing off with in 1996, because it had virtually no loft?

36. Which golfer hit Ben Crenshaw in the head with a putter in 1986, that forced Crenshaw to go to the hospital?

37. Which Japanese golfer is the only player to have won events on the Japanese, European, PGA, Senior and Australian Tours?

38. How many consecutive Majors had Tom Watson played until a shoulder injury forced him to miss the 1996 British Open?

a. 54   b. 60   c. 74   d. 87

39. Jack Nicklaus turned pro in 1961 and had a stellar career, winning a tournament in nearly every year that he played. When did he have his first winless year?

a. 1974   b. 1977   c. 1979   d. 1982

40. True or false: if a ball marker might interfere with play, then a player is allowed to move the ball marker out of their way if it is their own ball marker.

41. Which golf movie starred Kevin Costner?

42. Which Callaway driver was released in 1991?

43. What colour driver has Bubba Watson used for quite some time?

44. Why do golfers remove their glove when they go to putt?

45. Who won the Tokyo 2020 (2021) Tokyo Olympics women's gold medal?

46. What is Lee Westwood's Ryder Cup record?
a. 24-15-9   b. 20-18-6   c. 16-16-14   d. 13-9-22

47. What score did Schauffele shoot when he won the 2020 Olympics?
a. -10   b. -13   c. -16   d. -18

48. Which golfer said, "the most important shot in golf is the next one"?

49. There were 8 male and female golfers that represented the United States at the 2020 Tokyo Olympics. How many of them can you name? (1 point for each)

50. What brand is Bryson DeChambeau's driver?

Golfing Nicknames

1. The Big Easy

2. Fuzzy

3. The Slammer

4. The Black Knight

5. The Hawk

6. Beef

7. Merry Mex

8. Boo

9. Ohio Fats

10. Boom Boom

11. The Squire

12. Aquaman

13. The Cheetah

14. Lefty

15. El Mecanico

16. Chippie

17. El Nino

18. Gentle Ben

19. Great White Shark

20. Monty

21. Mad Scientist

22. Shrek

23. Wild Thing

24. Zinger

25. Wee-Mac

Guess the countries with the most golf courses

Number of courses	Country
15047	
3349	
2295	
2290	
1591	
637	
485	
484	
457	

444

418

410

383

316

The aim of this gmae is to get as few points as possible.

You get 0 points if you get the right country in the correct position. If your answers are 1 away then you get 1 point and so forth.

So, if you put Thailand for number 1, and it was actually number 7, then that would be 7 points.

If you put an answer that isn't on the list, then you get the maximum 15 points.

Jordan Spieth

1. In which year did Jordan Spieth turn professional?
a. 2009   b. 2010   c. 2011   d. 2012

2. As of August 2021, how many wins does Spieth have on the PGA Tour?
a. 12   b. 13   c. 14   d. 15

3. Which Major has Spieth never won as of August 2021?

4. Which of these events was Spieth's first win on the PGA Tour?
a. The Honda Classic   b. RBC Heritage
c. John Deere Classic   d. Arnold Palmer Invitational

5. Which pair did Jordan Spieth beat by 1 stroke to win the 2015 U.S Open?
a. Jason Day and Justin Rose
b. Rory McIlroy and Adam Scott
c. Dustin Johnson and Louis Oosthuizen
d. Phil Mickelson and Paul Casey

6. What is Jordan Spieth's career low round?
a. 60   b. 61   c. 62   d. 63

7. To the nearest million, what is Jordan Spieth's career prize money as of August 2021?
a. $28 million   b. $38 million   c. $48 million

8. At which course did Spieth win the 2015 U.S Open?

9. In which year did Spieth win his first PGA event?
a. 2011   b. 2012   c. 2013   d. 2014

10. Spieth had his best year to date in 2015. How many PGA Tour titles did he get in this year?
a. 4   b. 5   c. 6   d. 7

11. Who is Jordan Spieth's clothing sponsor?

12. What sport did Spieth originally love?

13. How old was Spieth when he played his first PGA event?

14. Who is Jordan Spieth's swing coach?

15. Who is Spieth's caddy?

16. How many birdies did Jordan get at the 2015 Masters?
a. 22   b. 25   c. 28   d. 31

17. Where did Spieth finish at his first Masters appearance?

18. What type of putting grip does Spieth use?

19. What brand of golf balls does Spieth use?

20. In which year was Spieth born?
a. 1990   b. 1991   c. 1992   d. 1993

Rory McIlroy

1. Where did McIlroy make his professional debut?
a. British Masters   b. Portugal Masters
c. Spanish Open   d. The Memorial Tournament

2. In which year did McIlroy turn pro?
a. 2005   b. 2006   c. 2007   d. 2008

3. Which tennis player did McIlroy become engaged to in 2011?

4. What is McIlroy's best finish at the Masters as of August 2021?

5. At which Ryder Cup did McIlroy make his Ryder Cup debut?
a. 2008 at Valhalla   b. 2010 at Celtic Manor
c. 2012 at Medinah   d. 2014 at Gleneagles

6. Who was McIlroy's first Ryder Cup partner?

7. Who was the opponent of McIlroy, when he famously nearly missed his tee time at the 2012 Ryder Cup?

8. Who did McIlroy defeat in a play-off at the 2016 Tour Championship to win the FedEx Cup?
a. Ryan Palmer   b. Ryan Moore   c. Ryan Fox

9. True or false: McIlroy currently has the most PGA Tour wins out of all the European golfers.

10. How many wins does McIlroy have on the PGA Tour?
a. 19   b. 23   c. 27   d. 31

11. What is McIlroy's career low round?
a. 60   b. 61   c. 62   d. 63

12. How many times has McIlroy won the FedEx Cup?
a. 1   b. 2   c. 3   d. 4

13. In which year did McIlroy win the U.S Open by 8 shots?
a. 2011   b. 2012   c. 2013   d. 2014

14. McIlroy also won another tournament by 8 shots. Which one was it?
a. 2012 PGA Championship   b. 2016 Tour Championship
c. 2015 AT&T Byron Nelson

15. Which player criticised McIlroy in 2011 after he skipped the Players Championship?

16. In which year did McIlroy win the Wells Fargo Championship?
a. 2012   b. 2014   c. 2019   d. 2021

17. When did McIlroy first become world number 1?
a. 2011   b. 2012   c. 2013   d. 2014

18. Which player finished runner up to McIlroy at the 2014 PGA Championship?
a. Phil Mickelson   b. Tiger Woods   c. Bubba Watson

19. Which Major has Rory won on multiple occasions?

20. How tall is McIlroy?
a. 5 ft, 8 in   b. 5ft, 9 in   c. 5ft, 10 in   d. 5ft, 11 in

Majors winners

1. Which 2 Majors has Collin Morikawa won?

2. Which Major did Jimmy Walker win in 2016?

3. Which 2 Majors did Angel Cabrera win?

4. Which Australian won the 2006 U.S Open?

5. In which year did Jim Furyk win the U.S Open?
a. 1995   b. 1999   c. 2003   d. 2006

6. How many Majors has Henrik Stenson won?

7. Who won the 2020 Open Championship?

8. Bernhard Langer won 2 Majors in his career. Which two did he win?

9. Which Major did Nick Faldo win first in 1987?

10. 2 consecutive Europeans won The Open Championship in 2018 and 2019. Who were they? (One point for each)

11. Who are the last 3 South Africans to win Majors? (1 point for every correct answer. and a bonus point if they are in the correct order)

12. In which year did Jason Day win the PGA Championship?
a. 2013   b. 2014   c. 2015   d. 2016

13. Which Major did Rich Beem win in 2002?

14. How many Majors did Hale Irwin win?
a. 1   b. 2   c. 3   d. 4

15. Who are the last 3 English golfers to win Majors as of August 2021? (1 point for every correct answer. and a bonus point if they are in the correct order)

16. Who are the last 3 Australian Major winners? (1 point for every correct answer. and a bonus point if they are in the correct order)

17. Which Major did Bryson DeChambeau win in 2020?

18. When did Vijay Singh win his last Major?
a. 2004   b. 2006   c. 2008   d. 2010

19. Which Major did Vijay Singh win twice?

20. Who are the last 3 Spanish Major winners? (1 point for every correct answer. and a bonus point if they are in the correct order)

21. Which 2 Majors has Zach Johnson won?

22. Who was the last Welshman to win Major?

23. Which golfer won the 1989 Open Championship?
a. Mark Calcavecchia   b. Curtis Strange   c. Tom Kite

24. In which year did Seve Ballesteros win his last Major?
a. 1985   b. 1986   c. 1987   d. 1988

25. When did the first Major begin?
a. 1850   b. 1855   c. 1860   d. 1865

26. The first Major to be held was the Open Championship. How many Scotsmen won it until a golfer from a different nation first won it?
a. 8   b. 14   c. 19   d. 29

27. As previously stated, the first Major to be held was The Open Championship. State the order that the next 3 would first appear on the Tour.

28. World War II had a big impact on the golfing Majors, resulting in many not being held. One of the Majors however was not so affected, and only missed one year in 1943. Which Major was this?

29. Matsuyama won the Masters in 2021. Who was the last man from Asia before Matsuyama to win a Major?

30. Who won the 2001 PGA Championship?
a. David Duval   b. David Toms   c. Steve Jones

Golfing Records

1. The current Guinness world record for the fastest round of golf was achieved by a South African golfer at Woodhill Golf Estate in Pretoria in 2008. The course is 6995 yards in length, and he shot 92. How long did it take him?
a. 15 mins 46 secs b. 22 mins 2 secs c. 26 mins 37 secs

2. Amazingly, the world longest drive was set in 1974. Even more surprising is that it was set by 64-year-old Mike Austin in the US National Seniors Tournament. How long was his drive?
a. 465 yards b. 485 yards c. 515 yards d. 530 yards

3. Which famous athlete (not necessarily a golfer) sunk the world's longest televised putt at the 2012 Dunhill Links Championship, when he holed a 159 foot putt?

4. Satsuki GC in Japan holds the record for the world's longest hole. It measures at a whopping 964 yards. What is par on this hole?
a. 5 b. 6 c. 7 d. 8

5. There have been 2 instances where a player has won the same golf tournament 8 times. Name the golfers and which tournament this was in.

6. There are 4 golfers with 14 or more consecutive seasons with a win to start their careers. Who are these golfers? (1 point for every correct answer)

7. Paul Lawrie holds the record for the largest final day comeback in a Major tournament. He achieved this at the 1999 Open Championship. How many strokes back was he?
a. 8   b. 9   c. 10   d. 11

8. Robert Gamez holds the record for the longest time between wins. This started at the Nestle Invitational and ended at the Valero Texas Open. How long was this streak?
a. 15 years 6 months   b. 17 years 9 months
c. 19 years 2 months   d. 23 years 3 months

9. Tiger Woods, Byron Nelson, Gene Sarazen, Walter Hagen and Tom Morris, Jr hold the record for the longest win streak in a single tournament. How long is this streak?
a. 4   b. 5   c. 6   d. 7

10. Bobby Locke, Sam Snead, Joe Kirkwood, Sr and J. Douglas Edgar share the record for the largest winning margin in a tournament. How large is this margin?
a. 14   b. 16   c. 18   d. 20

11. Corey Pavin holds the record for the lowest 9-hole score in a Major tournament at the 2006 U.S. Bank Championship in Milwaukee. The course par was 34, but what did he get?

12. Paul Gow and Mark Calcavecchia hold the record for the most birdies in a 72-hole event. How many birdies did they achieve?
a. 24   b. 28   c. 32   d. 36

13. Which former world number 1 holds the record for the lowest 72-hole round score of 253. which he achieved at the 2017 Sony Open in Hawaii?
a. Lee Westwood   b. Justin Thomas   c. Rory McIlroy
d. Luke Donald

14. Which golfer spent the most consecutive weeks at number 1 in the FedEx Cup? He achieved this in 2014.

15. Horton Smith holds the record for the most wins by players before the age of 23. Which current golfer is second on that list?

16. There have been 3 fathers and sons who have won the same tournament as each other. The last to achieve this were the Haas family who both won the Bob Hope Classic. What are the full names of the father and the son?

17. There has only been one grandfather and grandson pairing to win on the PGA Tour. The grandfather was Mike Turnesa whose first win came in 1931, but who was his grandson?

18. Sam Snead holds the record as the oldest player to finish in the top 10 in the official world rankings. How old was he?
a. 56 years 2 months   b. 59 years 7 months
c. 63 years 4 months   d. 67 years 2 months

19. Geoff Maggert holds the record for the most albatrosses in Majors. How many albatrosses did he get?
a. 2   b. 3   c. 4   d. 5

20. Ever since the PGA Tour started tracking hole-by-hole, 2 players have achieved the most holes-in-one. This has been achieved by Robert Allenby and Hal Sutton, but how many did they get?

a. 8   b. 10   c. 12   d. 14

Phil Mickelson

1. In which year did Phil Mickelson turn pro?
a. 1984   b. 1987   c. 1989   d. 1992

2. What score did Mickelson win the 2021 PGA Championship with?
a. -4   b. -6   c. -8   d. -10

3. Which 2 players finished runner up to Mickelson at the 2021 PGA Championship? (1 point for each)

4. What is Mickelson's Ryder Cup record?
a. 16-14-18   b. 23-12-16   c. 18-22-7   d. 27-14-7

5. How many Ryder Cup appearances has Mickelson made?
a. 8   b. 10   c. 12   d. 14

6. What is Mickelson's biggest winning margin?
a. -9   b. -11   c. -13   d. -15

7. Mickelson missed the cut at the 2014 Masters for the first time since when?
a. 1994   b. 1997   c. 2000   d. 2004

8. Which school did Mickelson attend?
a. Florida State   b. Stanford   c. UCLA   d. Arizona State

9. In which year did Mickelson win his first Major?
a. 2002   b. 2003   c. 2004   d. 2005

10. What was the first Major that Mickelson won?

11. Phil collapsed on the final hole of the 2006 US Open, when he needed a 4 for the win, 5 for the playoff and ended up shooting a 6. Who won the tournament instead?
a. Jim Furyk   b. Tiger Woods   c. Geoff Ogilvy

12. Who did Mickelson finish runner-up to at the 2013 US Open?

13. True or false: Mickelson won a PGA Tour event before he turned pro.

14. When did Mickelson first qualify for the U.S Ryder Cup team?
a. 1993   b. 1995   c. 1997   d. 1999

15. Who is Mickelson's club sponsor?

16. How many titles has Mickelson won on the PGA Tour?

17. To the nearest 1 million, what is Mickelson's career prize money?
a. $60 million   b. $78 million   c. $95 million

18. Out of the 650 events that Mickelson has played, how many cuts has he made?
a. 460   b. 492   c. 530   d. 563

19. Mickelson won 4 PGA Tour events in his best year. When did this occur?
a. 1996   b. 2001   c. 2005   d. 2011

20. What is Mickelson's career low round?
a. 60   b. 61   c. 62   d. 63

Answers

Warm up round

Majors	Nationality	Turned Pro	Name
18	United States	1961	Jack Nicklaus
15	United States	1996	Tiger Woods
11	United States	1912	Walter Hagen
9	United States	1919	Ben Hogan
9	South Africa	1953	Gary Player
8	United States	1971	Tom Watson
7	United States	1954	Arnold Palmer
7	United States	1931	Sam Snead
7	United States	1920	Gene Sarazen
7	United States	Never	Bobby Jones
7	United States	1890	Harry Vardon
6	England	1976	Nick Faldo
6	United States	1992	Phil Mickelson
6	United States	1960	Lee Trevino

Warm up round

Majors	Nationality	Turned Pro	Name
5	Spain	1974	Seve Ballesteros
5	United States	1932	Byron Nelson
5	Australia	1950	Peter Thomson
5	England	1890	J.Taylor
5	Scotland	1896	James Braid
4	United States	1961	Raymond Floyd
4	South Africa	1989	Ernie Els
4	United States	Never	Bobby Jones
4	South Africa	1938	Bobby Locke
4	Northern Ireland	2007	Rory McIlroy
4	United States	2012	Brooks Koepka

Ryder Cup

1. Abe Mitchell
2. 1927
3. 1979
4. Seve Ballesteros and Antonio Garrido
5. Fred Couples
6. Martin Kaymer
7. Ben Krenshaw
8. Nick Faldo
9. Arnold Palmer
10. Bill Rogers
11. Celtic Manor
12. Valhalla Golf Club
13. Ben Crenshaw
14. Ian Poulter and Paul Casey
15. Constantino Rocca
16. 1987
17. Paul Casey
18. 1993
19. 1989
20. Phillip Price
21. Brian Barnes

22. Seve Ballesteros & Jose Maria Olazabal

23. 4

24. Hal Sutton

25. 0

26. Ray Floyd

27. PGA national

28. 1983

29. Phil Mickelson

30. Sergio Garcia

31. Bernhard Langer

32. 19

33. David Gilford

34. 4

35. Dustin Johnson, Zach Johnson and Jason Dufner

36. Nick Faldo

37. Nicolas Colsaerts

38. Paul McGinley

39. 8.5

40. Thomas Pieters

Augusta

1. Horton Smith
2. 12th
3. Crow's nest
4. 3
5. He won with a score over par (+1)
6. Eisenhower
7. Faldo and Willett
8. Left handers
9. 2011
10. Angel Cabrera in 2009
11. Amen corner
12. Cameron Smith
13. 6
14. False, Tiger Woods has never led after the first round
15. 1949
16. A pair of crystal goblets
17. 75
18. Jack Nicklaus (6), Tiger Woods (5), Arnold Palmer (4), Jimmy Demaret (3), Sam Snead (3), Gary Player (3), Nick Faldo (3), Mickelson (3)

19. Seve Ballesteros

20. Phil Mickelson

21. Greg Norman

22. Sandy Lyle

23. Matt Kuchar

24. 6

25. Canada

26. 5

27. 22

28. The Palm

29. McDonalds

30. Farm

31. 3

32. 14

33. Oldest ever player to win the Masters

34. 5

35. 10th

36. 2005

37. Chris DiMarco

38. -10

39. Vijay Singh

40. -20

Tiger Woods

1. Eldrick Tont Woods
2. 15
3. 10
4. 11-1
5. Billy Mayfair
6. 5th
7. David Love III
8. 2001
9. Bay Hill
10. Phil Mickelson
11. Trevor Immelman
12. 1992 Genesis Open
13. Pebble Beach
14. 61
15. 7, and Byron Nelson with 11
16. 683 weeks
17. 2005 At&T Byron Nelson
18. 1 week
19. 80
20. PGA Championship

21. 1997
22. 18
23. 82
24. 24
25. Greg Norman
26. 22.8%
27. 121 million
28. 44-2
29. 4
30. 4

Golf Terminology

1. Albatross
2. Borrow
3. Fore
4. Stymie
5. Vardon grip
6. Carry
7. Honour
8. A scratch golfer
9. Ace
10. Mulligan
11. Greenkeeper
12. Break
13. Links
14. Stableford
15. Scramble
16. Texas Scramble
17. Skins
18. Lie
19. Backswing
20. Chunk

Guess the Golfer

1. Jon Rahm
2. Abraham Ancer
3. David Duval
4. Xander Schauffele
5. Hal Sutton
6. Tyrrell Hatton
7. Vijay Singh
8. Tony Finau
9. Marc Leishman
10. Jim Furyk
11. Curtis Strange
12. Viktor Hovland
13. Jesper Parnevik
14. Justin Thomas
15. Harris English
16. Paul Azinger
17. Stewart Cink
18. Mark O'Meara
19. Patrick Cantlay
20. Nick Price

21. Patrick Reed
22. Webb Simpson
23. Lee Westwood
24. Si Woo Kim
25. Will Zalatoris
26. Thomas Bjørn
27. Payne Stewart
28. Jason Kokrak
29. Sungjae Im
30. Corey Conners

Anagram Round

1. Jon Rahm
2. Abraham Ancer
3. Matt Fitzpatrick
4. Cameron Smith
5. Bryson DeChambeau
6. Greg Norman
7. Ernie Els
8. Brooks Koepka
9. Collin Morikawa
10. Fred Couples
11. Nick Faldo
12. Dustin Johnson
13. Jose Maria Olazabal
14. Louis Oosthuizen
15. Rory McIlroy
16. Vjay Singh
17. Jack Nicklaus
18. Hideki Matsuyama
19. Xander Schauffele
20. Tiger Woods

Anagrams of famous golf courses

1. St Andrews
2. Pine Valley
3. Augusta National
4. Cypress Point
5. Shinnecock Hills
6. Royal County Down
7. Oakmont Country
8. Muirfield
9. Merion
10. Pinehurst

General Knowledge

1. The Masters
2. Francesco Molinari
3. 3 mins
4. 14
5. Luke Donald and Lee Westwood
6. True
7. The general area, teeing areas, penalty areas, bunkers and putting greens
8. 1904
9. Rory McIlroy
10. Shane Lowry
11. The Players
12. $15 million
13. Shaun Micheel
14. 12
15. Sandwich
16. Scotland
17. Gene Sarazen (1935), Bruce Devlin (1967), Jeff Maggert, (1994), Louis Oosthuizen (2012)
18. 1552
19. Tony Jacklin

20. Dustin Johnson, Rory McIlroy, Justin Rose, Adam Scott, Lee Westwood, Sergio Garcia, Phil Mickelson, Rickie Fowler, Matt Kuchar, Louis Oosthuizen

21. Colin Montgomerie

22. South Africa

23. Ye Yang

24. 1. Tiger Woods = 41
    2. Ernie Els = 28
    3. Miguel Angel Jimenez = 21
    4. Padraig Harrington = 15

25. Jack Nicklaus (1971, '73), Tiger Woods (2000, '05)
    Rickie Fowler (2014), Jordan Spieth (2015)
    Brooks Koepka (2019)

26. Jose Maria Olazabal (Masters)
    Payne Stewart (US Open)
    Paul Lawrie (Open)
    Tiger Woods (PGA Championship)

27. England = Danny Willett (2016 Masters)
    Australia = Jason Day (2015 PGA Championship)
    South Africa = Ernie Els (2012 Open)
    Northern Ireland = Rory McIlroy (2014 PGA Championship)
    USA = Gary Woodland (2019 US Open)

28. Australia

29. Branden Grace

30. Annika Sorenstam

31. Chi Chi Rodriguez

32. 6th

33. The Masters

34. 3

35. 0

36. Trick question it was Ben Crenshaw himself

37. Isao Aoki

38. 87

39. 1979

40. True

41. Tin Cup

42. Big Bertha

43. Pink

44. They believe they have better feel

45. Nelly Korda

46. 20-18-6

47. -18

48. Ben Hogan

49. Justin Thomas, Collin Morikawa, Xander Schauffele, Patrick Reed, Nelly Korda, Danielle Kang, Lexi Thompson and Jessica Korda

50. Cobra

Golfing Nicknames

1. Ernie Els
2. Frank Urban Zoeller
3. Sam Snead
4. Arnold Palmer
5. Ben Hogan
6. Andrew Johnston
7. Lee Trevino
8. Thomas Brent Weekley
9. Jack Nicklaus
10. Fred Couples
11. Gene Sarazen
12. Woody Austin
13. Dustin Johnson
14. Phil Mickelson
15. Miguel Angel Jimenez
16. Paul Lowrie
17. Sergio Garcia
18. Ben Crenshaw
19. Greg Norman
20. Colin Montgomerie
21. Bryson Dechambeau

22. Louis Oosthuizen
23. John Daly
24. Paul Azinger
25. Rory McIlroy

Guess the countries with the most golf courses

Number of courses	Country
15047	United States
3349	United Kingdom
2295	Canada
2290	Japan
1591	Australia
637	France
485	Sweden
484	South Africa
457	Ireland

444	South Korea
418	Spain
410	New Zealand
383	China
316	Argentina

Jordan Spieth

1. 2012
2. 12
3. PGA Championship
4. John Deere Classic
5. Dustin Johnson and Louis Oosthuizen
6. 61
7. $48 million
8. Chambers bay
9. 2013
10. 5
11. Under Armour
12. Baseball
13. 16
14. Cameron McCormick
15. Michael Greller
16. 28
17. 2nd
18. Cross Handed
19. Titleist
20. 1993

Rory McIlroy

1. British Masters
2. 2007
3. Caroline Wozniaki
4. 4th
5. 2010 at Celtic Manor
6. Graeme McDowell
7. Keegan Bradley
8. Ryan Moore
9. True
10. 19
11. 61
12. 2
13. 2011
14. 2012 PGA Championship
15. Phil Mickelson
16. 2021
17. 2012
18. Phil Mickelson
19. PGA Championship
20. 5ft, 10 in

Majors Winners

1. 2021 Open Championship and the 2020 PGA Championship
2. PGA Championship
3. 2007 U.S Open and the 2009 Masters
4. Geoff Ogilvy
5. 2003
6. 1
7. Trick question, no one won it due to Covid
8. 1985 and 1993 Masters
9. The Open Championship
10. 2018 - Francesco Molinari, 2019 - Shane Lowry
11. Ernie Els - 2012 Open Championship,
    Charl Schwartzel - 2011 Masters,
    Louis Oostuizen - 2010 Open Championship
12. 2015
13. PGA Championship
14. 3
15. Danny Willett - 2016 Masters
    Justin Rose - 2013 U.S Open
    Nick Faldo - 1996 Masters

16. Jason Day - 2015 PGA Championship
    Adam Scott - 2013 Masters
    Geoff Ogilvy - 2006 U.S Open
17. U.S Open
18. 2004
19. PGA Championship
20. Jon Rahm - 2021 U.S Open
    Sergio Garcia - 2017 Masters
    Jose Maria Olazabal - 1999 Masters
21. 2015 Open Championship and the 2007 Masters
22. Ian Woosnam - 1991 Masters
23. Mark Calcavecchia
24. 1988
25. 2860
26. 29
27. U.S Open 1895, PGA Championship 1916, The Masters 1934
28. PGA Championship
29. Yang Yong-eun - 2009 PGA Championship
30. David Toms

Golf Records

1. 26 minutes 37 seconds
2. 515 yards. In this case distance was not everything though because Austin went 50 yards too long on a 450-yard par 4, and eventually 3 putted to make a 5.
3. Michael Phelps
4. 7
5. Trick question - they were both Tiger Woods World Golf Championships-Bridgestone Invitational and Arnold Palmer Invitational presented by MasterCard
6. Jack Nicklaus - 17 wins
   Arnold Palmer - 17 wins
   Tiger Woods - 14 wins
   Dustin Johnson - 14 wins   (active)
7. 10
8. 15 years 6 months
9. 4
10. 16
11. 26
12. 32
13. Justin Thomas
14. Jimmy Walker

15. Jordan Spieth
16. Jay Haas (father) and Bill Haas (son)
17. Marc Turnesa
18. 63 years 4 months
19. 2
20. 10

Phil Mickelson

1. 1992
2. -6
3. Louis Oostuizen and Brooks Koepka
4. 18-22-7
5. 12
6. -13
7. 1997
8. Arizona State
9. 2004
10. The Masters
11. Geoff Ogilvy
12. Justin Rose
13. True
14. 1995
15. Callaway
16. 45
17. $95 million
18. 530
19. 1996
20. 60

Printed in Great Britain
by Amazon

81843123R00052